Languages of the World

Italian

Sarah Medina

Raintree

www.raintreepublishers.co.uk
Visit our website to find out
more information about
Raintree books.

To order:
☎ Phone 0845 6044371
📄 Fax +44 (0) 1865 312263
🖳 Email myorders@raintreepublishers.co.uk

Customers from outside the UK please telephone +44 1865 312262

Raintree is an imprint of Capstone Global Library Limited,
a company incorporated in England and Wales having its
registered office at 7 Pilgrim Street, London, EC4V 6LB –
Registered company number: 6695582

Edited by Dan Nunn, Rebecca Rissman, and Catherine Veitch
Designed by Marcus Bell
Picture research by Ruth Blair
Originated by Capstone Global Library
Printed and bound in China by South China Printing
    Company Ltd

ISBN 978 1 406 22732 1 (hardback)
15 14 13 12 11
10 9 8 7 6 5 4 3 2 1

ISBN 978 1 406 22735 2 (paperback)
16 15 14 13 12
10 9 8 7 6 5 4 3 2 1

British Library Cataloguing in Publication Data
Medina, Sarah
Italian. -- (Languages of the world)
450-dc22
A full catalogue record for this book is available from the
British Library.

Acknowledgements
We would like to thank the following for permission to
reproduce photographs: Alamy pp. 5 (© dbimages), 21
(© Richard Broadwell), 22 (© Christine Webb), 25 (© Philip
Scalia); Corbis pp. 7 (© Image Source), 23 (© GAETAN
BALLY/Keystone), 24 (© Matthew Ashton/AMA), 26
(© A. Green); Shutterstock pp. 6 (© Oliver-Marc Steffen),
8 (© VolkOFF-ZS-BP), 9 (© blueking), 10 (© LeventeGyori),
11 (© Sarii Iuliia), 12 (© Andresr), 13 (© David Kelly),
14 (© Doreen Salcher), 15 (© ShopArtGallery),
16 (© Tulchinskaya), 17 (© Bernad), 18 (© Brian K.),
19 (© Petr Jilek), 20 (© ARENA Creative), 27 (© Dima
Fadeev), 28 (© Orange Line Media), 29 (© Tupungato).

Cover photograph of an adolescent girl reproduced with
permission of Getty Images (Marcy Maloy).

We would like to thank Nino Puma for his invaluable help in
the preparation of this book.

Contents

Italian words are in italics, *like this*. You can find out how to say them by looking in the pronunciation guide.

Italian around the world

Italian is the main language of most people in Italy and San Marino. Some people in Malta, Switzerland, Vatican City, Croatia, Slovenia, Monaco, Albania, and Tunisia speak Italian, too.

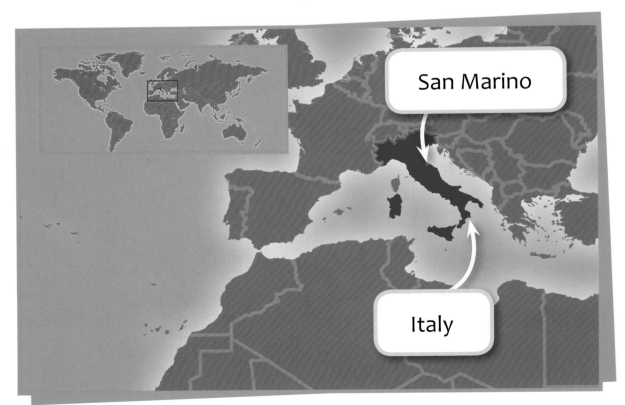

San Marino

Italy

Many people in the United States speak Italian.

Italian is also spoken by some people in many other countries around the world – from France in Europe to the United States in North America, and Brazil in South America.

Who speaks Italian?

Italian is the main language of about 60 million people. However, up to 90 million other people around the world can speak Italian, too. Italian is one of the world's top 20 most spoken languages.

In Tuscany, *cola* sounds like "hola"!

In different parts of Italy the way that people speak Italian varies a lot. The letter "c" is usually sounded, or pronounced, like a "k", but in Tuscany people pronounce it like an "h".

Italian and English

Some words, such as *pizza* and *piano*, are the same in Italian and English. Other words are very similar. Can you guess the meaning of the words below?

bicicletta   *studente*   *pinguino*   *famiglia*

(See page 32 for answers.)

English uses Italian words for different types of pasta, such as *spaghetti* and *maccheroni*!

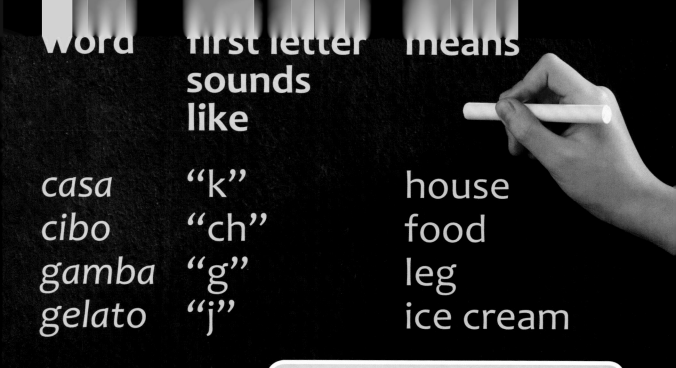

word	first letter sounds like	means
casa	"k"	house
cibo	"ch"	food
gamba	"g"	leg
gelato	"j"	ice cream

> The same letter in Italian can have more than one sound.

Some letters in Italian have different sounds. The letter "c" can sound like a "k" or like "ch". The letter "g" can sound like a "g" in "good" or like a "j".

Learning Italian

Italian uses the same alphabet as English. However, unlike English, in Italian the letters j, k, w, x, and y are not used very often. They are mainly used in words that come from other languages.

These are the main letters in the Italian alphabet
abcdefghilmnopqrstuvz

These letters are not used very often
jkwxy

The word *pésca* means "fishing" in Italian, but *pèsca* means "peach"!

The Italian language uses special marks called accents to make vowels have different sounds. An acute accent looks like this: ´. A grave accent looks like this: `.

Saying hello and goodbye

Family and friends usually give each other a kiss on each cheek when they greet each other. People who do not know each other normally shake hands.

How to say it
handshake = *stretta di mano*
kiss = *bacio*

How to say it
good morning = *buongiorno*
hello = *ciao*
goodbye = *addio or ciao*

In Italian people often say "*buongiorno*" to say "hello" and "*addio*" to say "goodbye". "*Ciao*" can mean either "hello" or "goodbye".

Talking about yourself

When people meet others for the first time they usually give their name. They may say *"Mi chiamo Sarah"*. *"Piacere"* means "Pleased to meet you."

How to say it
My name is …
= *Mi chiamo* …
Pleased to meet you
= *Piacere*

How to say it

I come from … = *Vengo dall'* …
Italian … = *Italiano* (boy) or *Italiana* (girl)
I live in … = *Abito a* …

People often say where they are from. For example, "*Vengo dall' Italia*" means "I come from Italy". They may say where they live. For example, "*Abito a Roma*" ("I live in Rome").

Asking about others

It is polite to ask other people about themselves. The first thing people usually ask is someone's name. They say, "*Come ti chiami?*"

How to say it
What's your name? = *Come ti chiami?*

How to say it
Where are you from? = *Di dove sei?*
Where do you live? = *Dove abiti?*

To ask someone where they are from, people usually say *"Di dove sei?"* If they want to know where someone lives, they say *"Dove abiti?"*

At home

In Italian cities most people live in apartments or flats instead of houses. Some apartment buildings are new, but many are very old.

How to say it
apartment = *appartamento*
house = *casa*

How to say it
farmhouse = *fattoria*
living room = *soggiorno*
kitchen = *cucina*
bathroom = *bagno*
swimming pool = *piscina*

In the countryside some families live in farmhouses. Some farmhouses are very large, with lots of rooms. Some even have a swimming pool!

19

Family life

In Italy, family is very important. In the south of the country parents, children, and grandparents often live together.

How to say it
mother = *madre*
father = *padre*
brother = *fratello*
sister = *sorella*

How to say it
family = *famiglia*
grandfather = *nonno*
grandmother = *nonna*

A popular activity in Italy is the *passeggiata*, when people take an evening stroll. Many families enjoy talking to each other, as well as meeting other people, during the *passeggiata*.

At school

Many Italian children go to school at half past eight. At half past one, they go home for lunch. However, they have to go to school from Monday to Saturday!

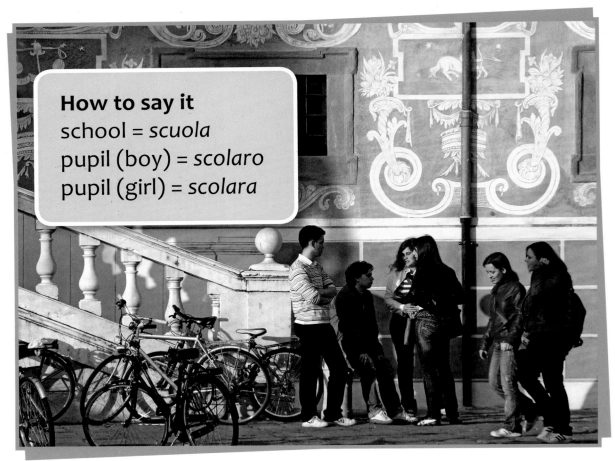

How to say it
school = *scuola*
pupil (boy) = *scolaro*
pupil (girl) = *scolara*

How to say it
science = *scienza*
art = *arte*
languages = *lingue*

Italian pupils can choose what type of secondary school they go to. Schools specialize in different subjects, such as science, art, or languages.

Sport

Football is the main sport in Italy.
All the big cities have their own football
team and stadium – and thousands
of fans!

How to say it
sport = *sport*
football = *calcio*
team = *squadra*
stadium = *stadio*

How to say it
ball = *palla*
bowls = *bocce*

Many people in Italy enjoy the game of *bocce*, which is a type of bowls. Two people, or two small teams, play against each other on special outdoor courts.

Food

In Italy, the main meal of the day is lunch. People often eat three courses: pasta, then meat with salad or vegetables, followed by fruit or dessert.

How to say it
lunch = *pranzo*
pasta = *pasta*
meat = *carne*
salad = *insalata*
vegetables = *verdure*
fruit = *frutta*
dessert = *dolce*

How to say it
Parmesan cheese = *Parmigiano*
olives = *olive*
olive oil = *olio d'oliva*
pizza = *pizza*

Many Italian foods are enjoyed around the world. People use Italian Parmesan cheese on pasta dishes. Some people enjoy Italian olives and olive oil. Pizza is popular everywhere!

Clothes

Many people in Italian-speaking countries relax in casual clothes like T-shirts and jeans. For work, people wear more formal clothes like suits, shirts, and skirts.

How to say it
T-shirt = *maglietta*
jeans = *jeans*
shirt = *camicia*
skirt = *gonna*

Most Italians love clothes. They are known for their good style. Some Italian fashion designers, such as Armani and Prada, are famous all over the world.

Pronunciation guide

English	Italian	Pronunciation
apartment	appartamento	a-par-ta-men-toh
art	arte	ahr-tay
ball	palla	pah-lah
bathroom	bagno	bah-nyo
bowls	bocce	bo-chay
brother	fratello	frah-tay-loh
designer	stilista	stee-lee-stah
dessert	dolce	dol-chay
family	famiglia	fah-mee-lee-yah
farmhouse	fattoria	fa-tour-ee-a
fashion	moda	moh-dah
father	padre	pah-dray
football	calcio	cahl-choh
fruit	frutta	froo-tah
goodbye	addio	a-deo
grandfather	nonno	noh-noh
grandmother	nonna	noh-nah
hello	ciao	chow
house	casa	cah-zah
I come from ...	Vengo dall' ...	Ven-go da
I live in ...	Abito a ...	Ah-bee-toh ah
Italian (boy)	Italiano	Ee-tah-lee-ah-noh
Italian (girl)	Italiana	Ee-tah-lee-ah-nah
Italy	Italia	Ee-tah-lee-ah
jeans	jeans	jeens
kitchen	cucina	koo-chee-nah

languages	*lingue*	*lin-goo*
living room	*soggiorno*	*soh-jor-noh*
lunch	*pranzo*	*prahn-tsoh*
meat	*carne*	*car-nay*
mother	*madre*	*mah-dray*
My name is ...	*Mi chiamo ...*	*Mee kee-ah-moh*
olive oil	*olio d'oliva*	*o-leo doh-lee-vah*
olives	*olive*	*oh-lee-veh*
Parmesan cheese	*Parmigiano*	*Par-mee-jah-noh*
pasta	*pasta*	*pah-stah*
pizza	*pizza*	*pee-tsah*
Pleased to meet you.	*Piacere.*	*Pee-ah-chay-ree*
pupil (boy)	*scolaro*	*s-co-la-row*
pupil (girl)	*scolara*	*s-co-la-ra*
Rome	*Roma*	*Roh-mah*
salad	*insalata*	*in-sah-lah-tah*
school	*scuola*	*skoo-oh-lah*
science	*scienza*	*shee-en-sah*
shirt	*camicia*	*cah-mee-tchah*
sister	*sorella*	*soh-ray-lah*
skirt	*gonna*	*goh-nah*
sport	*sport*	*spohrt*
stadium	*stadio*	*stah-dee-oh*
suit	*vestito*	*vay-stee-toh*
swimming pool	*piscina*	*pee-shee-nah*
team	*squadra*	*skwah-drah*
T-shirt	*maglietta*	*mah-lee-ay-tah*
vegetables	*verdure*	*vayr-doo-ray*
What's your name?	*Come ti chiami?*	*Coh-may tee kee-ah-me?*
Where are you from?	*Di dove sei?*	*Dee doh-vay say?*
Where do you live?	*Dove abiti?*	*Doh-vay ah-bee-tee?*

Find out more

Books

Country Topics: Italy, R. Wright (Franklin Watts, 2007)
Oxford First Italian Words, David Melling (OUP, 2009)
We're From Italy, Vic Parker (Heinemann, 2006)

Websites

kids.nationalgeographic.com/kids/places/find/italy/
www.pocanticohills.org/italy/italy.htm

Index

Meaning of the words on page 8

bicicletta	= bicycle	*pinguino*	= penguin
studente	= student	*famiglia*	= family